j 355.7 GOL
Goldsworthy, Steve.
Pentagon

PENTAGON

Steve Goldsworthy

www.av2books.com

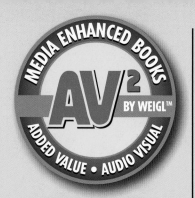

AV² provides enriched content that supplements and complements this book. Weigl's AV² books strive to create inspired learning and engage young minds in a total learning experience.

Your AV² Media Enhanced books come alive with...

Audio
Listen to sections of the book read aloud.

Key Words
Study vocabulary, and complete a matching word activity.

Video
Watch informative video clips.

Quizzes
Test your knowledge.

Go to **www.av2books.com**, and enter this book's unique code.

BOOK CODE

K 1 7 4 3 4 3

Embedded Weblinks
Gain additional information for research.

Slide Show
View images and captions, and prepare a presentation.

AV² by Weigl brings you media enhanced books that support active learning.

Try This!
Complete activities and hands-on experiments.

... and much, much more!

Published by AV² by Weigl
350 5th Avenue, 59th Floor
New York, NY 10118

Website: www.av2books.com   www.weigl.com

Library of Congress Cataloging-in-Publication Data

Goldsworthy, Steve.
 Pentagon / Steve Goldsworthy.
    p. cm. -- (Virtual field trip)
 Includes index.
 ISBN 978-1-61913-254-2 (hardcover : alk. paper) -- ISBN 978-1-61913-260-3 (pbk)
 1. Pentagon (Va.)--Juvenile literature. I. Title.
 UA26.A745G65 2012
 355.709755'295--dc23
                        2011045454

Printed in the United States of America in North Mankato, Minnesota
1 2 3 4 5 6 7 8 9 0 16 15 14 13 12

012012
WEP060112

Editor: Heather Kissock
Design: Terry Paulhus

Every reasonable effort has been made to trace ownership and to obtain permission to reprint copyright material. The publishers would be pleased to have any errors or omissions brought to their attention so that they may be corrected in subsequent printings.

Weigl acknowledges Getty Images as its primary image supplier for this title.

Contents

What is the Pentagon?

The Pentagon is one of the most recognizable buildings in the United States. Located in Arlington County, Virginia, it has been the headquarters for the United States Department of Defense since 1943. At 6.6 million square feet (613,140 square meters), its unique five-sided, or pentagonal, design houses the largest office space in the world.

Construction of the structure began on September 11, 1941. Three months later, the Japanese attacked Pearl Harbor, a major U.S. Navy base in Hawai'i. This attack plunged the United States into World War II. These events accelerated the construction of the Pentagon. Within five months, 1 million square feet (92,903 sq. m) of offices were available for personnel of the War Department. The building was completed in just 16 months at a total cost of more than $83 million.

The Pentagon stood strong for many years. Then, on September 11, 2001, terrorists crashed an airliner into the building's west side. More than 150 people were killed in the attack. In the following months, the damaged areas were rebuilt. The Pentagon once again stands as a symbol of U.S. strength.

The Pentagon has three times more floor space than the Empire State Building in New York City.

Snapshot of Virginia

Virginia is located in the northeast United States. The Atlantic Ocean serves as its eastern border. Maryland and the District of Columbia (D.C.) sit to its north and east. It shares its southern border with Tennessee and North Carolina, its western border with Kentucky, and West Virginia sits to its northwest.

INTRODUCING VIRGINIA

CAPITAL CITY: Richmond

FLAG:

MOTTO: *Sic Semper Tyrannis* (Thus Always to Tyrants)

NICKNAME: Old Dominion

POPULATION: 8,001,024 (2010)

ADMITTED TO UNION: June 25, 1788

CLIMATE: Subtropical, with four distinct seasons

SUMMER TEMPERATURE: Average of 79° Fahrenheit (26° Celsius)

WINTER TEMPERATURE: 40°F (4°C)

TIME ZONE: Eastern Standard Time (EST)

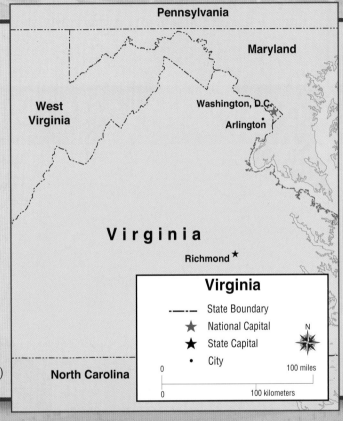

Pennsylvania

Maryland

West Virginia

Washington, D.C.

Arlington

Virginia

Richmond ★

Virginia

- – – State Boundary
- ★ National Capital
- ★ State Capital
- • City

N

| 0 | | 100 miles |

| 0 | | 100 kilometers |

North Carolina

Virginia Symbols

Virginia has several official symbols. Some symbols represent the features that distinguish the area from other parts of the United States. Others indicate details about the state's history.

OFFICIAL FLOWER
Dogwood

OFFICIAL BIRD
Cardinal

OFFICIAL TREE
Scarlet Oak

OFFICIAL INSECT
Tiger Swallowtail Butterfly

A Step Back in Time

During World War I, the United States War Department was spread out among 17 buildings throughout Maryland, Virginia, and the District of Columbia. Its headquarters was the **Munitions** Building, in Washington, D.C. When World War II broke out in Europe in 1939, the U.S. War Department anticipated the country's eventual involvement in the conflict and decided to expand. A new building began construction in Washington, D.C., but the War Department outgrew the building before it was completed.

CONSTRUCTION TIMELINE

AD 1918
The Main Navy and Munitions Buildings are constructed in Washington, D.C., as temporary quarters for the United States Military.

July 17, 1941
The War Department assigns an architect and engineer to design its new building.

August 14, 1941
Congress approves funding for the construction of the Pentagon.

September 11, 1941
Construction of the Pentagon officially begins.

After the Pentagon was built, the Munitions Building housed part of the Navy's operations. The building was demolished in 1970.

More than 15,000 construction workers helped build the Pentagon. At one point, there were three rotating shifts of personnel working 24 hours a day.

In May 1941, the Secretary of War, Henry L. Stimson, had an important meeting with President Franklin D. Roosevelt. He spoke about the War Department's need to be under one roof. The U.S. government spent the next several months considering various locations for the new structure. It finally decided on a site in Arlington, Virginia.

Franklin Delano Roosevelt was the 32nd president of the United States. He served four terms, from 1933 to 1945.

December 7, 1941
The Japanese attack Pearl Harbor, sending the United States into World War II.

April 30, 1942
Employees begin moving into the Pentagon.

January 14, 1943
The Pentagon officially opens.

September 11, 2001
Terrorists crash an airplane into the Pentagon's west side. Rebuilding begins shortly after.

August 15, 2002
The west side reopens.

The 9/11 terrorists crashed an airplane through three of the Pentagon's five rings.

The Pentagon Location

The site of the Pentagon had to be considered very carefully. It had to be close to the rest of the government buildings, yet have its own space and room to grow. Several locations were surveyed in and around Washington, D.C. Finally, the government chose an area across the Potomac River from Washington, D.C. in Arlington, Virginia.

This site was not the first choice. The government first considered a plot of land called Arlington Farms. The new building was even designed as a pentagon to take the shape of the land. This site was rejected, however. It was too close to Arlington National Cemetery, where many U.S. presidents and war heroes are buried.

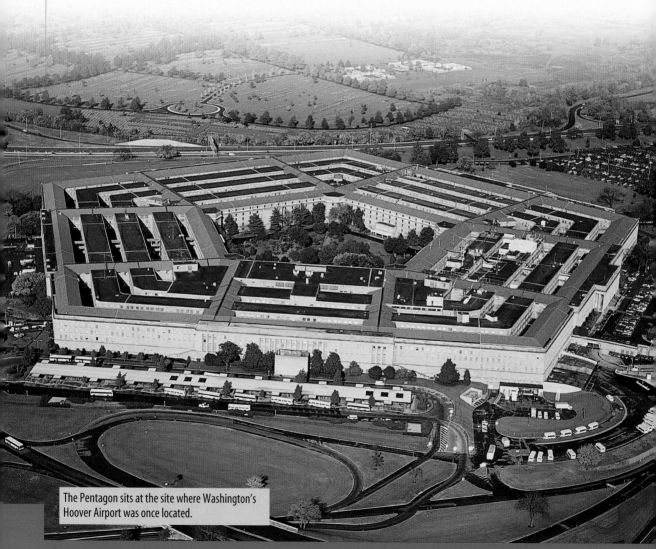

The Pentagon sits at the site where Washington's Hoover Airport was once located.

The Pentagon Today

As a structure, the Pentagon remains much the same as it was when it was built 70 years ago. In 2011, however, major **renovations** were completed to bring the building up to modern standards. These included upgrading windows and doors, and increasing security for the Pentagon's more than 26,000 employees.

Height and Length The Pentagon is 77 feet (23 m) tall. Each of the five sides of the building is 921 feet (281 m) long.

Area The structure occupies 1.3 million square feet (120,770 sq. m) of land, with 217,800 square feet (20,234 sq. m) for the central courtyard.

217,800 square feet (20,234 sq. m)

77 feet (23 m)

921 feet (281 m)

Materials The **foundation** of the Pentagon consists of 41,492 concrete **piles**. The entire structure is made from more than 435,000 cubic yards (333,000 cubic meters) of concrete.

Outside the Pentagon

The overall design of the Pentagon is one based on simplicity and security. It was so simple it took architects and designers only 34 days to come up with the initial design.

Exterior Walls Unlike other government buildings, there is very little decorative work on the outer walls. Instead, the limestone walls are finished in a smooth, **classical** style. The exterior walls of the Pentagon are divided into five **façades**.

Most U.S. government buildings are made from marble. Limestone was used on the Pentagon because it was available locally. Marble comes from Italy, which was an enemy of the United States during World War II.

In 2006, the military observed the fifth anniversary of the 2001 terrorist attack with a ceremony on the Mall Terrace.

Mall Terrace Entrance The north side of the structure is called the Mall **Terrace** Entrance façade. The small terrace is used for ceremonies throughout the year. The entrance features a **portico** held up by several columns. The Mall Terrace Entrance is the public entrance to the Pentagon.

The River Terrace was the site of a farewell ceremony for the outgoing Secretary of Defense, Robert Gates, in 2011.

River Terrace Entrance Continuing clockwise around the building is the River Terrace Entrance façade. It overlooks a **lagoon** and the city of Washington, D.C. Another terrace leads down to the lagoon and a landing platform. This platform was originally used as a dock for boats ferrying military personnel from nearby Bolling Air Force base to the Pentagon.

The Pentagon Memorial features a park with 184 benches. Each bench represents one of the victims of the attack.

Heliport

The Heliport façade is located on the west side of the building. People arriving at the Pentagon by helicopter land by this façade. It was the Heliport façade that was hit during the 2001 terrorist attacks. Today, a memorial to the victims of the attack has been built on the land adjacent to the façade.

South Parking Entrance

On the southwest side of the building is the South Parking Entrance façade. This is where the Pentagon's main parking lot is found. As a result of the activity, this façade has several loading platforms and entrances for cars and other vehicles.

There is no public parking at the Pentagon. All of the spaces are for people working at the Pentagon.

Concourse Entrance

The Concourse Entrance façade is found on the southeast side of the building. Like all of the façades, it features a **colonnade**. Situated in the middle of the wall, the colonnade consists of 16 rectangular columns that stretch three stories in height. The Concourse Entrance is where the Pentagon Metro rail station and bus station are located.

The Pentagon Metro station opened on July 1, 1977. At the time, it had a direct entrance to the Pentagon. After the 2001 terrorist attack, this entrance was closed.

Inside the Pentagon

The interior of the Pentagon has many features that make it appear like its own town. With so many people working inside, steps have been taken to make sure their needs are met.

Floor Plan Most of the Pentagon's floor space is taken up by offices. These offices are located throughout five aboveground floors and two basement levels. Each floor has five, **concentric** hallways that are linked by 10 other hallways. There are more than 17.5 miles (28 km) of hallways in the Pentagon.

Due to the arrangement of the hallways in the Pentagon, it takes no longer than seven minutes to walk from one part of the building to another.

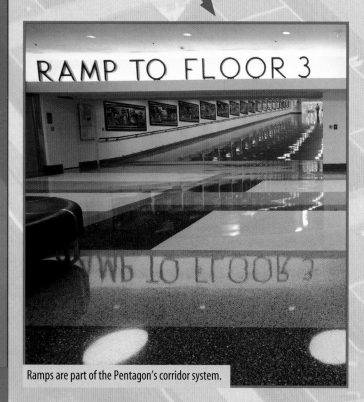

Ramps are part of the Pentagon's corridor system.

Ramps Ramps are used to connect the various levels of the building. The initial design for the Pentagon did not include elevators. The metal needed to make them was needed for the war effort. As well, the building planners decided that stairs would be too inefficient for people to move from floor to floor. Dozens of concrete ramps were incorporated to make it easier to move not only people but equipment and materials. In recent years, eight passenger elevators have been added to the Pentagon.

The Chapel features a stained-glass window that pays tribute to those who died in the 2001 attack.

Chapel The Chapel is dedicated to those who lost their lives on September 11, 2001. It is located at the exact point where the airliner crashed into the building. Nearby is the America's Heroes Memorial. The memorial pays tribute to those who lost their lives in the tragedy.

Shopping and Restaurants The Pentagon has a shopping area located on the second floor of the Concourse Entrance. The mini-mall has several shops and services, including a hair salon, shoe repair booth, and dozens of stores. There is also a food court and several restaurants. This shopping area is only accessible to personnel working at the Pentagon. There are additional shops open to the public in other areas.

The Pentagon food court features many well-known fast food outlets.

Central Courtyard In the outdoor center of the Pentagon is a 217,800 square foot (20,234 sq. m) area known as the Central Courtyard. It is a park-like setting, with trees, benches, and picnic tables. People come to the Central Courtyard to take coffee and lunch breaks. The courtyard even has a public restaurant, aptly named the Center Courtyard Cafe.

VIRTUAL TOUR

The Pentagon has 4,200 clocks, 19 escalators, 691 water fountains, 284 restrooms, 1 dining room, 2 cafeterias, and 6 snack bars.

Military demonstrations are sometimes held in the Central Courtyard.

Big Ideas Behind the Pentagon

The people who designed the Pentagon had to consider many factors. They had to consider the building's location and what type of land it would sit on. This information helped the designers determine the layout of the building and the materials that would be used to construct it.

Keeping the building low helped preserve the view from Arlington National Cemetery.

Loads

A load is a force that impacts how a structure must be built. Designers and **architects** must consider loads when planning a building. There are two types of loads. The dead load is the weight of the building itself. The live load is the weight of the building with its contents, including people. The Pentagon was built on a **floodplain**. The land on a floodplain can be unstable due to the movement of water. As a result, the ground could only support a building that was low to the ground. To make the building the needed size, architects decided to spread the structure out over the land.

Reinforced Concrete

Most of the Pentagon was constructed from reinforced concrete. Concrete is known for its strength and ability to stand up to many of the conditions a building will experience. It takes a long time to show signs of wear and is resistant to freezing and thawing. Concrete is also watertight. All of these **properties** made it a good material to use in the construction of the Pentagon. Concrete itself easily resists compression, or squeezing. However, it does not stand up to tension, or pulling, very well. For this reason, steel bars were added to the concrete to build the Pentagon. This is called reinforced concrete and is much stronger than either concrete or steel alone.

To reinforce concrete, metal bars are placed inside the concrete mold. As the concrete dries, the bars bond to it.

Science at Work in the Pentagon

At the time of the Pentagon's construction, no one had attempted building such a huge structure. Architects had to employ science to solve many of the project's challenges.

Pile drivers drop weight onto the pile, driving it into the ground. This work is similar to hitting a nail with a hammer.

Hydraulics

When the foundation for the Pentagon was being built, workers drove a series of piles into the ground to provide support for the building. They used machines called pile drivers to do this work. Many pile drivers use a hydraulic system to provide the force needed to get the piles into the ground. A hydraulic system has two **pistons** in cylinders filled with an **incompressible** liquid, often oil. The pistons are connected by a pipe. When pressure is applied to one piston, the force is transferred to the second piston through the oil. As one piston is pushed down, the other is lifted up by the oil. This movement is used to raise a striker, which then falls, driving the pile into the ground.

Pulleys

Lifting the heavy concrete into place required the use of construction cranes. Cranes rely on a simple machine called a pulley to lift heavy objects. A pulley is a freely turning wheel with a grooved rim over which a cable is guided.

A hook can be added to a pulley system to raise and lower objects.

An object that needs to be moved is attached to one end of the cable. The other end of the cable is then pulled, and the object is lifted. The wheel changes the direction of force. This allows the load to be lifted to great heights by applying force to the rope at the ground level.

VIRTUAL TOUR

About 680,000 tons (616,885 tonnes) of sand and gravel were used to make the concrete needed to build the Pentagon.

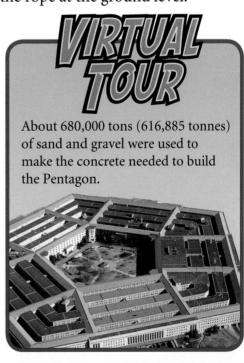

The Pentagon Builders

The design and construction of the Pentagon, like most structures, took the combined efforts of many men and women. Architects, planners, and **engineers** designed the structure, while thousands of workers built it.

Following his retirement, Brehon Somervell was promoted to the rank of four-star general. This is one of the highest positions in the military.

Brigadier-General Brehon Somervell
Head of Construction, U.S. Army

At the time of the Pentagon's construction, the War Department's construction chief was General Brehon Somervell. Somervell was an accomplished engineer. He was known in the military for his ability to get building projects done on time and under budget. His bravery and engineering skills during World War I earned him both the Distinguished Service Medal and the Distinguished Service Cross. He was appointed as head of the Construction Division in December 1940. Soon after, he was assigned the job of coordinating the construction of the Pentagon.

Lieutenant-Colonel Hugh Casey
Chief of Design and Engineering, U.S. Army

Hugh Casey worked for General Somervell in the Construction Division. When the division received approval to begin constructing a building for the War Department, Somervell gave Casey the

Prior to the Pentagon project, Hugh Casey had been heavily involved in the construction of several dams and flood control systems.

job of creating the building's design. Casey worked with George Bergstrom to develop the basic design of the building. This design came together over a weekend. Bergstrom then began developing the details of the design.

George Bergstrom Architect

American architect George Bergstrom was hand-picked by General Somervell to design the Pentagon. George Bergstrom had attended Yale University and received a Bachelor of Science degree from the Massachusetts Institute of Technology in 1899. He spent many years designing everything from movie theaters to public schools. He was serving as the president of the Southern California chapter of the American Institute of Architects when he was recruited for the Pentagon job.

George Bergstrom designed part of the Hotel Alexandria, in Los Angeles, California.

Concrete Finishers

The Pentagon project employed thousands of concrete finishers. These construction workers pour, place, and finish concrete. Concrete is a material made up of cement, granite, and sand. The Pentagon construction workers dredged up 680,000 tons (616,885 tonnes) of sand and gravel from the nearby Potomac River to make the 435,000 cubic yards (332,581 cu. m) of concrete required for the Pentagon. With the exception of the external wall, most of the Pentagon is made of concrete.

After the concrete is poured, concrete finishers spread it to the desired thickness.

Interior Designers

Interior designers plan the interior of a building. They supervise the selection of office furniture, carpets, and paint. They also design staff kitchen areas and waiting rooms. The Pentagon's designers were concerned not with how beautiful the inside of the building was, but how functional it needed to be.

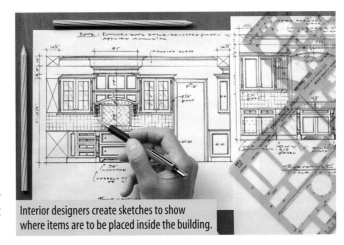

Interior designers create sketches to show where items are to be placed inside the building.

Structural Engineers

Structural engineers study the architect's design and work out the details needed to bring the design into reality. Their job relies mainly on a knowledge of science principles involved in carrying loads. The structural engineer makes sure that the building will hold together under its weight, the weight of everything in it, and the forces that work against it. They inspect the building at different stages of the process to make sure the structure can withstand forces, such as wind, rain, and vibration. Engineers are people who develop safe and cost-effective ways of solving problems.

Structural engineers often work with architects, construction workers, and other engineers.

Similar Structures Around the World

The Pentagon's design and size make it one of the most unique and recognizable buildings in the world. There are really no other buildings quite like it. There are, however, some similar structures.

Beijing National Stadium

BUILT: 2008
LOCATION: Beijing, China
DESIGN: Jacques Herzog and Pierre de Meuron
DESCRIPTION: Like the Pentagon, the Beijing National Stadium was a low-rise building designed to sustain massive weight in a circular layout. The building was created for the 2008 Summer Olympics. Like the Pentagon, the main structure is a giant concrete bowl. This structure, however, is surrounded by an outer steel frame. The structure has the nickname "The Bird's Nest" as the steel exterior looks like a collection of giant twigs.

The Palace of Parliament covers an area of 3.5 million square feet (325,000 sq. m). It cost about $3 billion to build.

The structure of the National Stadium is composed of two independent elements. One is the steel legs, and the other is the concrete bowl. Each stands 50 feet (15.2 m) apart from the other.

Palace of the Parliament

BUILT: 1984
LOCATION: Bucharest, Romania
DESIGN: Anca Petrescu
DESCRIPTION: The Palace is the workplace of the Romanian Parliament. It is listed in the Guinness Book of World Records as the largest and most expensive civilian administrative building in the world. It is also the heaviest building.

JPMorgan Chase Tower

BUILT: 1982
LOCATION: Houston, Texas, United States
DESIGN: I.M. Pei & Partners
DESCRIPTION: At 1,002 feet (305 m), the JPMorgan Chase Tower is the tallest five-sided, or pentagonal-shaped, building in the world. The western corner of the tower has been "sheared off" to form the unique five-sided shape. This west side of the tower is covered by a wall of glass that runs the entire height of the building, 75 stories. This "fifth wall" was designed to give people an uninterrupted view of the city of Houston.

The Sky Lobby on the JPMorgan Chase Tower's 60th floor offers the public the highest view of Houston.

The Fortress of Bellegarde is located on the border between France and Spain.

Fortress of Bellegarde

BUILT: 17th century
LOCATION: Roussillon, France
DESIGN: Marshal Vauban
DESCRIPTION: The **fortress** was originally a fortified tower. The walls of the structure are a series of concentric pentagons, just like the Pentagon. Bellegarde even has a pentagonal courtyard. The fort held an important military position, protecting France from neighboring Spain.

Issues Facing the Pentagon

There are many issues facing the structure of the Pentagon. Structural issues due to the age of the building are creating environmental issues. As with most government buildings, there is also the constant threat of violence against the building and the people inside.

WHAT IS THE ISSUE?

Many of the Pentagon's systems, such as the electrical, plumbing, heating, and ventilation, have become outdated.

Military efforts are not always popular with the public. Many protests against the actions of the U.S. military have taken place in front of the Pentagon.

EFFECTS

Old materials and ineffective office renovations have made the Pentagon an inefficient and sometimes unhealthy place to work.

Security continues to be a priority at the Pentagon, both for its personnel and the protection of military **intelligence**.

ACTION NEEDED

Major renovations were completed that included the removal of harmful **asbestos** in the walls, rewiring, plumbing upgrades, and a change to **open concept** office spaces.

The Department of Defense created the Pentagon Force Protection Agency to deal with potential threats. Construction continues to reinforce the outer walls of the Pentagon.

Make a Pentagram Pentagon

Geometry is an area of mathematics that relates to lines, angles, and points. You can use geometry to create a perfect pentagon. An easy way to make a pentagon is to start with a star. The geometric term for a five-pointed star shape is a pentagram. Try this geometric activity to explore the relationship between a pentagram and a pentagon.

Materials
- sheet of paper
- pencil
- geometry compass
- ruler
- protractor
- scissors

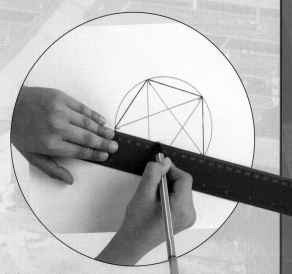

Instructions
1. Mark a dot in the middle of your piece of paper. Using the geometry compass, draw a perfect circle around the dot.

2. Use the ruler to draw a horizontal line across your circle and directly through the center dot.

3. Put the protractor on the line. Keep in mind that a pentagram is divided into five equal parts. A circle is made up of 360 degrees. When 360 is divided by 5, the result is 72. Using your protractor, mark a point on the 0 degree of your circle. Mark the next point at the 72 degree of your circle. Mark another point at the 144 degree point, and two other marks at the 216 degree and 288 degree points of your circle. If using the half-circle protractor, flip your circle over to mark all five points. After this is done, erase the horizontal line.

4. Draw a straight line from the point at the top center of your circle down to the bottom left "corner" of your circle. Draw another line straight down from your top center point to the bottom right "corner." Draw a line across your circle from the outer left and right points. Then, draw a line from the outer left point to the bottom right "corner." Finally, draw a line from the outer right point to the bottom left "corner." You should now have a perfect five-pointed star, or pentagram.

5. Use your scissors to cut off the "arms" of the star. You should now be left with only the pentagon inside.

Pentagon Quiz

Q On what date did construction of the Pentagon begin?

A September 11, 1941

Q Where did the War Department originally plan to build the Pentagon?

A At Arlington Farms

Q How tall is the Pentagon?

A 77 feet (23 m)

Q Which side of the Pentagon serves as the public entrance?

A The Mall Terrace Entrance

Words to Know

architects: people who design buildings

asbestos: a highly toxic heat-resistant fiber that was used in floors, walls, and insulation

classical: relating to ancient Greece or Rome

colonnade: a series of columns

concentric: circles that share the same center

congress: the national legislative, or law-making, body of a country. In the U.S., it is made up of the Senate and the House of Representatives

engineers: people who design, build, or maintain things

façades: any side of a building that faces a public space

floodplain: land bordering a river that is prone to flooding

fortress: a military stronghold often protected by high walls

foundation: the base on which something stands

incompressible: impossible to make smaller

intelligence: secret information about enemies, spies, etc.

lagoon: an artificial pool

munitions: war materials such as weapons and ammunition

open concept: having few or no internal walls

piles: heavy beams driven into the ground to provide support for a building

pistons: disks that fit into a cylinder and move under fluid pressure

portico: a covered porch

properties: qualities or attributes

renovations: the results of restoring something to its original form or remodeling it

terrace: a platform or walkway extending outside

Index

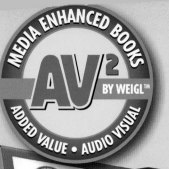

Log on to www.av2books.com

AV² by Weigl brings you media enhanced books that support active learning. Go to www.av2books.com, and enter the special code found on page 2 of this book. You will gain access to enriched and enhanced content that supplements and complements this book. Content includes video, audio, weblinks, quizzes, a slide show, and activities.

Audio
Listen to sections of
the book read aloud.

Video
Watch informative video clips.

Embedded Weblinks
Gain additional information
for research.

Try This!
Complete activities and
hands-on experiments.

WHAT'S ONLINE?

Try This!	**Embedded Weblinks**	**Video**	**EXTRA FEATURES**
Identify the features of the Pentagon.	Find out more about the Pentagon.	Watch a video to learn how to make an origami pentagon.	
Imagine that you are designing the Pentagon.	Learn about the design and construction of the Pentagon.	Watch a video to learn more about the memorial at the Pentagon.	
Test your knowledge of the Pentagon.	Play games to learn more about geometry.	Take a video tour of the Pentagon Memorial.	

 Audio
Listen to sections of
the book read aloud.

 Key Words
Study vocabulary, and
complete a matching
word activity.

 Slide Show
View images and captions
and prepare a presentation

 Quizzes
Test your knowledge.

AV² was built to bridge the gap between print and digital. We encourage you to tell us what you like and what you want to see in the future.

Sign up to be an AV² Ambassador at www.av2books.com/ambassador.